A MONSTER CALLED DEPRESSION

INT PRODUCTION

In the shadows of the human mind, lurks a silent monster that does not distinguish between ages, genders or social status. A monster that can paralyze, consume and darken even the sunniest days. That monster is called depression.

Depression is one of the most common and debilitating mental illnesses in today's society, affecting millions of people around the world. Often misunderstood and underestimated, depression is not simply feeling sad or discouraged; It is a complex disorder that affects the way a person thinks, feels and behaves.

In this book, we will explore the depths of this monster called depression, unraveling its roots, its manifestations and its consequences in the lives of those who suffer from it. Through real stories, scientific data and practical advice, we will seek to shed light on this disease, break down stigmas and offer supportive guidance for those fighting it.

It's time to face the monster, to talk openly and honestly about depression, to seek help and understanding, and to remember that hope and recovery are possible. Join me on this journey to understand and fight together this invisible but devastating monster that threatens the mental health of so many.

Together, we can challenge this monster called depression and build a path to healing and hope. Because depression does not define who suffers from it, and every story of struggle is a testimony of courage and resistance.

1.1 WHAT IS DEPRESSION?

Depression is a mood disorder that affects the way a person thinks, feels and behaves, and can significantly interfere with their ability to function in daily life. It is characterized by a persistent feeling of sadness, hopelessness, apathy, and lack of interest in activities that were previously pleasurable.

Depression can manifest itself in various forms and degrees of severity, from mild and transient episodes to chronic and debilitating disorders. Some of the common symptoms of depression include:

- Feelings of sadness, emptiness or hopelessness.

- Loss of interest or pleasure in daily activities.

- Changes in appetite or weight.

- Sleep problems, such as insomnia or excessive sleeping.

- Fatigue or lack of energy.

- Feelings of guilt or worthlessness.

- Difficulty concentrating or making decisions.

- Thoughts of death or suicide.

It is important to note that depression is not simply feeling sad from time to time, but involves a constellation of symptoms that persist for   an extended period of time and negatively affect the quality of life of the person experiencing it.

Depression is a serious and debilitating mental illness, but it is treatable. There are different treatment approaches, which may include psychological therapy, antidepressant medications, lifestyle changes, and social support. Seeking professional help is essential to manage depression effectively and regain emotional and mental well-being.

If you think you or someone you know may be experiencing depression, it is important to seek help from a mental health professional to receive an accurate diagnosis and appropriate treatment plan. You are not alone in this battle, and recovery is possible with the right support.

1.2 IMPORTANCE OF THE TOPIC

The importance of the issue of depression lies in its profound and widespread impact on people's mental health and quality of life. Below are some key reasons that highlight the relevance of tackling depression effectively:

1. **Prevalence:** Depression is one of the most common mental illnesses worldwide, affecting people of all ages, genders and ethnic groups. Its prevalence has increased significantly in recent decades, making it a major public health problem.

2. **Impact on quality of life:** Depression can have a devastating impact on the quality of life of those who suffer from it, affecting their ability to work, study, maintain healthy relationships and enjoy everyday activities. It can lead to feelings of hopelessness, social isolation, physical health problems, and in extreme cases, suicidal thoughts.

3. **Economic and social costs:** Depression not only affects the individual, but also has a significant impact on the economy and society in general. Costs associated with depression include health care expenses, loss of work productivity, work absenteeism, and emotional and financial burden on families and communities.

4. **Stigma and lack of awareness:** Despite its high prevalence, depression remains stigmatized in many societies, which can make it difficult for people to seek help and access effective treatments. Lack of awareness and understanding of depression can perpetuate the suffering of those who suffer from it and make timely prevention and treatment difficult.

5. **Possibility of treatment and recovery:** Despite the severity of depression, it is important to note that it is treatable. There are effective interventions, such as psychological therapy, antidepressant medications, lifestyle changes and social support, that can help people manage their symptoms and regain their emotional and mental well-being.

Depression is an issue of great importance due to its widespread impact, its implications on quality of life, its economic and social burden, the associated stigma and the need for awareness, understanding and support for those who suffer from it. Addressing depression effectively is essential to promoting mental health, preventing unnecessary suffering, and providing hope and help to those in need.

1.3 O BJECTIVES OF THE BOOK

1. **Raise awareness:** Inform readers about what depression is, its symptoms, causes, effects and how it affects those who suffer from it, as well as demystify misconceptions and stigmas associated with this disease.

2. **Provide educational information:** Provide detailed and accurate information about depression, including statistical data, scientific research, types of depression, risk factors, and available diagnosis and treatment methods.

3. **Provide Support and Hope:** Offer practical advice, coping strategies, helpful resources, and inspiring testimonies to those struggling with depression, as well as their families and loved ones.

4. **Promote prevention:** Educate about the risk factors for depression, the early signs of the disease and the preventive measures that can be taken to reduce the risk of developing depression or to detect and treat it early.

5. **Promote empathy and understanding:** Help readers better understand what it is like to live with depression, encourage empathy towards those who suffer from it, and promote open and respectful dialogue about mental health in society.

6. **Inspire to action:** Motivate readers to seek professional help if they are experiencing symptoms of depression, to support those who suffer from it, to promote mental health in their communities, and to contribute to the reduction of the stigma associated with mental disorders.

7. **Provide a resource guide:** Include a list of helpful resources, such as helplines, mental health organizations, recommended books, mobile apps, and specialized websites, so readers can access additional support and continue your path to recovery and well-being.

CA CHAPTER 2

DEPRESSION IN CURRENT SOCIETY

In today's society, depression is an increasingly relevant and worrying mental health problem due to several factors that influence its prevalence and its impact on people's lives. Below are some characteristics of how depression manifests itself in contemporary society:

1. **Fast-paced lifestyle:** In the age of technology and rapid information, many people experience high levels of stress, work pressure, lack of time for self-care and difficulties disconnecting, which can contribute to development of depression.

2. **Social Isolation:** Despite digital connectivity, many people feel lonely, disconnected and lack meaningful social relationships, which can increase the risk of depression and other mental health problems.

3. **Pressure for success and image:** In a society obsessed with perfection, performance and personal image, unrealistic expectations can lead to feelings of incompetence, low self-esteem and anxiety, risk factors for depression.

4. **Impact of Social Media:** While social media can be a powerful tool for connection and communication, it can also contribute to negative comparisons,   cyberbullying , addiction to external validation and the feeling of not measuring up, all of which can affect mental health.

5. **Economic and work problems:** Job instability, unemployment, job insecurity, pressure to perform and the lack of balance between work and personal life can be triggering factors of depression in today's society.

6. **Limited access to mental health services:** Despite advances in mental health awareness, many people face barriers to accessing quality mental health services, which can include high costs, stigma, lack of resources and long waiting lists.

7. **Impact of traumatic events and global crises:** Natural disasters, economic crises, social conflicts and pandemics such as COVID-19 can increase stress, anxiety and depression at the individual and collective levels, exacerbating the challenges of mental health in society.

2.1 FACTORS THAT CONTRIBUTE TO DEPRESSION

Depression is a complex illness that can be caused by a combination of biological, genetic, psychological and environmental factors. Below are some of the factors that can contribute to the development of depression:

1. **Biological factors**: Chemical imbalances in the brain, such as low levels of serotonin, norepinephrine, and dopamine, may play a role in the development of depression.

2. **Genetic factors**: Depression can be hereditary. People with a family history of depression have a higher risk of developing it.

3. **Psychological factors**: Traumatic experiences, abuse, stressful events, low self-esteem, relationship problems, and personality disorders can contribute to the development of depression.

4. **Environmental factors**: Factors such as the loss of a loved one, financial problems, work problems, significant life changes, social isolation, and other stressors can trigger depression.

5. **Physiological factors**: Chronic illnesses, chronic pain, hormonal imbalances, and other physical health problems can contribute to the development of depression.

6. **Social and cultural factors**: Culture, social environment, lack of support from friends and family, discrimination and other social factors can influence depression.

2.2 STATISTICS AND RELEVANT DATA OF DEPRESSION

Depression is a common mental disorder worldwide that affects people of all ages. Here are some relevant statistics and facts about depression:

1. **Prevalence**: Depression is one of the leading causes of disability worldwide. According to the World Health Organization (WHO), it is estimated that more than 264 million people worldwide suffer from depression.

2. **Economic impact**: Depression has a great economic impact. Depression and other mental disorders are estimated to cost the global economy more than $1 trillion a year in lost productivity.

3. **Suicide**: Depression is a major risk factor for suicide. It is estimated that approximately 60-70% of people who commit suicide suffer from depression or some other mood disorder.

4. **Gender**: Women are more likely to experience depression than men. This gender disparity may be due to biological, social and cultural factors.

5. **Age**: While depression can affect people of all ages, it is most common in young and middle-aged adults. However, children, adolescents, and older adults can also experience depression.

6. **Treatment**: Although depression is highly treatable, it is estimated that less than half of people with depression worldwide receive adequate treatment. There are various treatment options, including psychological therapy, antidepressant medication, and other therapeutic approaches.

2.3 STIGMA AND PREJUDICES

Stigma and prejudice related to mental health, including depression, are common in many societies and can make it difficult for people to seek help and treatment. Here are some examples of stigma and prejudice associated with depression:

1. **Social stigma**: There is a social stigma around mental disorders, including depression. People can be stigmatized, judged or   marginalized for their mental health condition, which can lead to discrimination and isolation.

2. **Lack of understanding**: Many people have a limited understanding of depression and other mental disorders, which can lead to misconceptions and prejudices. This can make it difficult for people with depression to feel understood and supported.

3. ** Self-stigma **: Social stigma can lead people to internalize feelings of shame, guilt, or self-stigma about their depression. This can make it difficult for them to seek help and treatment, as they may feel that they will be judged or stigmatized by others.

4. **Impact on Help Seeking**: Stigma can be a significant barrier to people seeking professional help for depression. Fear of rejection, discrimination, or judgment from others can lead people to avoid talking about their mental health and seek treatment.

5. **Inadequate treatment**: The stigma associated with depression can lead to people receiving inadequate or insufficient treatment. Lack of social support and discrimination can make it difficult for people to access effective treatment options.

3. CHAPTER 3

TYPES OF DEPRESSION

There are several types of depression, each with its own characteristics and symptoms. Below are some of the most common types of depression:

1. **Major depression**: Also known as major depressive disorder, it is the most common form of depression. It is characterized by symptoms such as deep sadness, loss of interest in pleasurable activities, changes in appetite and sleep, fatigue, feelings of guilt, and suicidal thoughts.

2. **Dysthymic disorder**: This is a chronic form of depression that is less severe than major depression, but persists for a long period of time, usually two years or more. Symptoms are less intense but may be persistent.

3. **Recurrent depressive disorder**: It is characterized by having recurrent episodes of major depression throughout a person's life. Depressive episodes may be separated by periods of time when the person feels normal or less depressed.

4. **Seasonal affective disorder**: This type of depression is related to seasonal changes, particularly winter, and manifests itself with depressive symptoms during certain times of the year.

5. **Persistent depressive disorder (dysthymia chronic)**: It is a form of chronic depression that lasts at least two years. The symptoms are less severe than in major depression, but they are persistent.

6. **Postpartum depression**: Occurs in women after childbirth and is characterized by symptoms of depression that may include sadness, fatigue, mood swings, difficulty sleeping, and problems bonding with the baby.

These are just some of the most common types of depression. Each person can experience depression uniquely, so it is important to seek help from a mental health professional for an accurate diagnosis and appropriate treatment.

3.1 MAJOR DEPRESSION

Major depression, also known as major depressive disorder or unipolar disorder, is a severe form of depression that significantly affects a person's daily life. Here is information about major depression:

Characteristics of major depression:

1. **Symptoms**: Major depression is characterized by a combination of emotional, physical and cognitive symptoms that persist for at least two weeks. Symptoms may include deep sadness, hopelessness, loss of interest or pleasure in daily activities, changes in appetite and weight, difficulty sleeping, fatigue, feelings of guilt or worthlessness, difficulty concentrating, and thoughts of death or suicide.

2. **Duration**: To be diagnosed with major depression, a person must experience these symptoms most of the day, almost every day, for at least two weeks.

3. **Impact on daily life**: Major depression can significantly interfere with a person's ability to function in their daily life.   It can affect interpersonal relationships, work or academic performance, and overall physical health.

4. **Treatment**: Major depression is treatable. Treatment may include psychological therapy (such as cognitive behavioral therapy), antidepressant medications, and lifestyle changes. The combination of therapy and medication is often effective in treating major depression.

5. **Suicide prevention**: It is important to note that major depression can increase the risk of suicide. If someone is showing signs of suicidal thoughts or suicidal behavior, it is crucial to seek professional help immediately.

6. **Social support**: Support from friends, family, and mental health professionals is essential to help people with major depression overcome this illness. Stigma and lack of understanding around depression can make it difficult for people to seek help, so awareness and education are important to combat this problem.

If you think you are experiencing symptoms of major depression, I recommend seeking help from a mental health professional to receive an accurate diagnosis and appropriate treatment plan. Major depression is a serious condition, but with the right support, many people can recover and lead full, satisfying lives.

3.2 DYSTHYMIC DISORDER

Dysthymic disorder, also known as dysthymic disorder or dysthymia , is a chronic, long-lasting mood disorder characterized by the presence of persistent but less severe depressive symptoms than those of major depression. Some important aspects of dysthymic disorder are:

1. **Duration**: To be diagnosed with dysthymic disorder, depressive symptoms must be present for most of the day, most days, for at least two years in adults (one year in adolescents and children). During this period, there may be brief periods of improvement, but the person is usually not completely free of symptoms.

2. **Symptoms**: The symptoms of dysthymic disorder are usually less intense than those of major depression, but they are persistent. Common symptoms include chronic sadness, hopelessness, lack of energy, low self-esteem, difficulty concentrating, changes in appetite or sleep, and a general feeling of being unwell.

3. **Impact on daily life**: Although the symptoms of dysthymic disorder may be less intense than those of major depression, they can still significantly affect a person's quality of life. It can interfere with work, interpersonal relationships, academic performance, and the ability to enjoy everyday life.

4. **Treatment**: Dysthymic disorder is treatable. Treatment may include psychological therapy, such as cognitive behavioral therapy, and in some cases, antidepressant medications. The combination of therapy and medication can be effective in helping people manage symptoms and improve their quality of life.

5. **Prevention of major depression**: Dysthymic disorder may increase the risk of developing major depression in the future. Therefore, it is important to seek treatment and support to address symptoms and prevent long-term complications.

3.3 DISORDER BI POLAR

Bipolar disorder, formerly known as manic-depressive illness, is a mood disorder characterized by extreme changes in mood, energy, and ability to function in daily life. Here is information about bipolar disorder:

Characteristics of bipolar disorder:

1. **Manic Episodes**: In bipolar disorder, people experience manic episodes, which are periods of extreme excitement, euphoria, increased energy, racing thinking, impulsive behavior, and lack of sleep. During manic episodes, a person may feel invincible, have grandiose ideas, and make risky decisions.

2. **Depressive episodes**: In addition to mania, people with bipolar disorder also experience depressive episodes, which are periods of deep sadness, hopelessness, fatigue, lack of interest in pleasurable activities, changes in appetite and sleep, suicidal thoughts and other depressive symptoms.

3. **Types of bipolar disorder**: There are several types of bipolar disorder, including bipolar disorder type I (characterized by full-blown manic episodes followed by depressive episodes), bipolar disorder type II (characterized by milder hypomanic episodes and depressive disorders), and cyclothymic disorder (a milder, more chronic form of bipolar disorder).

4. **Causes**: Although the exact cause of bipolar disorder is not completely known, it is believed that genetic, biological, environmental and psychological factors may contribute to the development of the disorder.

5. **Treatment**: Bipolar disorder is a chronic but treatable condition. Treatment usually includes a combination of mood-stabilizing medications, psychological therapy (such as cognitive behavioral therapy), stress management, regular exercise, adequate sleep, and social support.

6. **Importance of diagnosis and treatment**: It is essential to obtain an accurate diagnosis and an appropriate treatment plan for bipolar disorder, as appropriate treatment can help people manage symptoms, prevent relapses, and lead a better life. full and productive.

3.3   POST-PARTUM DEPRESSION

Postpartum depression is a medical condition that affects some women after giving birth. It is characterized by feelings of sadness, anxiety, extreme tiredness, and hopelessness that can make it difficult to care for the baby and the mother's daily functioning.

Some common symptoms of postpartum depression include drastic mood swings, frequent crying, difficulty sleeping even when the baby is sleeping, lack of interest in activities you used to enjoy, feelings of worthlessness or guilt, difficulty concentrating, loss of appetite, or increased appetite. himself, among others.

It is important for any woman experiencing these symptoms to seek help immediately. Postpartum depression is treatable and there are various treatment options, which may include psychological therapy, antidepressant medications, support from family and friends, and lifestyle changes.

CHAPTER 4

4.1 CAUSES AND RISK FACTORS

Depression is a multifactorial disease that can be caused by a combination of biological, genetic, psychological and environmental factors. Some of the possible causes and risk factors for depression include:

1. **Biological factors:** Imbalances in certain neurotransmitters in the brain, such as serotonin, norepinephrine, and dopamine, may play a role in the development of depression. Changes in the functioning of certain areas of the brain can also influence.

2. **Genetic factors:** There is evidence that depression may have a genetic component. People with a family history of depression have a higher risk of developing the disease.

3. **Psychological factors:** Traumatic experiences, chronic stress, low self-esteem, persistent negative thoughts, interpersonal conflicts and other psychological factors can contribute to the development of depression.

4. **Environmental factors:** Stressful events such as the loss of a loved one, financial problems, job problems, major life changes, physical or emotional abuse, and other traumatic events can trigger or contribute to the development of depression.

5. **Hormonal factors:** Changes in hormonal levels, such as those that occur during pregnancy, postpartum, menopause or as a result of endocrine disorders, can influence the onset of depression.

6. **Medical illnesses:** Some medical conditions, such as chronic illnesses, chronic pain, heart disease, cancer, diabetes, and thyroid disorders, can increase mental illnesses

4.1 BIOLOGICAL FACTORS

Biological factors that can influence the development of depression include:

1. **Brain chemical imbalances:** It has been observed that imbalances in the activity of neurotransmitters such as serotonin, norepinephrine and dopamine may be associated with depression. These neurotransmitters play an important role in regulating mood, and their alteration may contribute to the development of the disease.

2. **Genetics:** There is evidence that genetic predisposition can influence a person's vulnerability to depression. Research suggests that certain genes may increase the risk of developing mood disorders, including depression.

3. **Brain structure and function:** Neurobiological studies have identified differences in brain structure and function in people with depression compared to those without depression. For example, brain regions such as the hippocampus, prefrontal cortex, and amygdala may show alterations in individuals with depression.

4. **Hormonal factors:** Changes in hormone levels, such as cortisol (the stress hormone), can influence the development of depression. Imbalances in the hypothalamic-pituitary-adrenal axis, which regulates the stress response, may play a role in the onset of depressive symptoms.

4.2 PSYCHOLOGICAL FACTORS

Psychological factors also play an important role in the development and manifestation of depression. Some of the psychological factors that can influence depression include:

1. **Traumatic experiences:** Traumatic events in a person's life, such as physical, emotional or sexual abuse, loss of a loved one, serious accidents or any other traumatic experience, can increase the risk of developing depression.

2. **Chronic stress:** Ongoing stress, whether due to work, family, financial situations, or other stressors, can contribute to the development of depression. Chronic stress can strain a person's emotional resources and increase vulnerability to mental health problems.

3. **Low self-esteem:** People with low self-esteem tend to have a negative view of themselves and the world around them, which can predispose them to depression. Excessive self-criticism and lack of self-confidence can be risk factors for the development of the disease.

4. **Persistent negative thoughts:** Negative thinking patterns, such as constant rumination about past negative events or anticipation of negative outcomes in the future, can contribute to the onset and maintenance of depression.

5. **Interpersonal conflicts:** Difficulties in interpersonal relationships, such as family conflicts, relationship problems, lack of social support or social isolation, can trigger or aggravate depression.

6. **Perfectionism:** The tendency to set excessively high standards and be self-demanding can increase the risk of depression, especially when achievements do not meet those unrealistically high expectations.

4.3 SOCIAL FACTORS

Depression is a complex illness that can be caused by a combination of biological, psychological and social factors. As for social factors that may contribute to the development of depression, here are some examples:

1. **Stressful life events**: Traumatic experiences, significant losses, family conflicts, work or financial problems can increase the risk of depression.

2. **Social isolation**: Lack of social support, loneliness and disconnection from others can be risk factors for depression.

3. **Interpersonal problems**: Conflicts in personal relationships, emotional or physical abuse, lack of close and supportive relationships can contribute to the development of depression.

4. **Social and cultural pressure**: Unrealistic social and cultural expectations, discrimination, social stigma, restrictive gender norms, among others, can influence mental health and contribute to depression.

5. **Socioeconomic conditions**: Poverty, lack of access to basic resources, unemployment and other unfavorable socioeconomic conditions can increase the risk of depression.

6. **History of trauma**: Traumatic experiences in childhood or adulthood, such as abuse, neglect, violence or natural disasters, can increase vulnerability to depression.

CHAPTER 5

SYMPTOMS OF DEPRESSION

Depression is a mood disorder that can affect a person's emotions, thinking, and behavior. Some of the common symptoms of depression include:

1. **Persistent feelings of sadness, anxiety, or emptiness**: A constant feeling of sadness, hopelessness, or apathy that does not go away.

2. **Loss of interest or pleasure in activities**: Loss of interest in activities that used to be pleasurable, including hobbies, socialization, and interpersonal relationships.

3. **Changes in appetite or weight**: Significant weight gain or loss for no apparent reason, or changes in appetite.

4. **Sleep disorders**: Insomnia, difficulty falling asleep or sleeping excessively.

5. **Fatigue or lack of energy**: Feeling of constant tiredness, lack of energy and difficulty carrying out daily activities.

6. **Feelings of guilt or worthlessness**: Persistent thoughts of guilt, worthlessness, or excessive self-criticism.

7. **Difficulty concentrating or making decisions**: Trouble concentrating, remembering details, or making decisions, even on simple tasks.

8. **Agitation or lethargy**: Restlessness, irritability or agitation, or, conversely, slowness in movements and speech.

9. **Thoughts of death or suicide**: Recurrent thoughts about death and suicide

5.1 PHYSICAL SYMPTOMS

In addition to emotional and behavioral symptoms, depression can also manifest with physical symptoms. Some of the physical symptoms that may be associated with depression include:

1. **Chronic pain**: Depression can be related to chronic pain, such as headaches, back pain, muscle aches, or other types of physical discomfort.

2. **Gastrointestinal problems**: Some people with depression may experience gastrointestinal symptoms, such as an upset stomach, nausea, diarrhea, or constipation.

3. **Fatigue and lack of energy**: Extreme fatigue and lack of energy are common symptoms in depression, which can make daily tasks more difficult to complete.

4. **Weight changes**: Depression can lead to changes in appetite and weight, which can result in significant weight loss or gain.

5. **Sleep problems**: Sleep disorders are common in depression, and can manifest as insomnia (difficulty falling asleep) or hypersomnia (excessive sleeping).

6. **Headaches**: Recurrent headaches or migraines may be associated with depression in some people.

7. **Back and neck problems**: Depression can contribute to muscle tension in the back and neck, which can result in chronic pain in these areas.

5.2 EMOTIONAL SYMPTOMS

Emotional symptoms are a fundamental part of depression, as this disorder significantly affects a person's mood and emotions. Some of the common emotional symptoms associated with depression include:

1. **Persistent feelings of sadness**: Deep, persistent, overwhelming sadness that does not seem to have a specific cause and is present most of the time.

2. **Feelings of hopelessness and helplessness**: Feeling that things will never get better, accompanied by a feeling of helplessness and hopelessness about the future.

3. **Irritability or agitation**: Feelings of irritability, frustration and agitation that can manifest as sudden mood changes or exaggerated reactions to everyday situations.

4. **Anxiety**: Excessive worry, nervousness and anxiety that may be present along with depression.

5. **Feelings of guilt or worthlessness**: Excessive self-criticism, feelings of guilt for no apparent reason, and a distorted perception of oneself as worthless or unworthy.

6. **Loss of interest or pleasure**: Inability to experience pleasure in activities normally enjoyed, which can lead to apathy and loss of interest in life.

7. **Feelings of emptiness**: Feeling of emotional emptiness, as if there were no positive emotions at all, even in the presence of pleasant events.

8. **Difficulty concentrating or making decisions**: Problems concentrating, remembering details or making decisions, which can interfere with daily and work activities.

9. **Thoughts of death or suicide**: Recurrent thoughts about death, self-destruction or suicide, as well as the feeling that the world would be better off without the   possibility of living

5.3 COGNITIVE SYMPTOMS

The cognitive symptoms associated with depression can affect the way a person thinks, processes information, and relates to themselves and the world around them. Some of the common cognitive symptoms of depression include:

1. **Persistent negative thoughts**: A negative and pessimistic view of yourself, others and the future, which can lead to a cycle of self-destructive thoughts.

2. **Difficulty concentrating**: Problems concentrating, maintaining attention, and processing information, which can interfere with the ability to perform everyday tasks.

3. **Mental rumination**: Tendency to ruminate or dwell on negative thoughts and worries repetitively, without finding solutions or relief.

4. **Excessive self-criticism**: Tendency to criticize oneself excessively and uncompassionately, developing a distorted and negative image of oneself.

5. **Memory loss**: Difficulty remembering information, recent events or important details, which can affect the ability to function in daily life.

6. **Slow or fuzzy thinking**: Feeling that your thinking is slower, fuzzy, or cloudy than usual, which can make everyday tasks more difficult to perform.

7. **Pessimism and lack of hope**: Constant feeling of hopelessness and lack of positive expectations about the future, which can interfere with motivation and the search for solutions to problems.

8. **Cognitive distortions**: Tendency to distort reality, interpreting information in a negative or exaggerated way, which can increase the feeling of hopelessness and helplessness.

CHAPTER 6

DIAGNOSIS AND TREATMENT OF L A   DEPRESSION

The diagnosis of depression is usually made through an evaluation by a mental health professional, such as a psychiatrist, psychologist, or family doctor. Diagnosis is based on a combination of physical, emotional and cognitive symptoms, as well as the duration and severity of symptoms. Some of the methods that can be used to diagnose depression include clinical interviews, self-assessment questionnaires, and observation of the patient's behavior.

Once a diagnosis of depression has been made, treatment may include a combination of psychological therapy, medications, and lifestyle changes. Here are some common treatment options for depression:

1. **Psychological therapy**: Cognitive behavioral therapy (CBT) is a commonly used approach to treating depression. There are also other forms of therapy, such as interpersonal therapy, supportive therapy, and acceptance and commitment therapy, that may be beneficial.

2. **Antidepressant medications**: In some cases, a doctor may prescribe antidepressant medications to help relieve symptoms of depression. These medications may include selective serotonin reuptake inhibitors (SSRIs), serotonin and norepinephrine reuptake inhibitors (SNRIs), and other types of antidepressants.

3. **Complementary Therapies**: Some people find relief in complementary therapies such as acupuncture, meditation, yoga or light therapy, especially in cases of seasonal depression.

4. **Social support**: Support from friends, family, and support groups can be essential in the treatment of depression, as it helps reduce isolation and provides an emotional support system.

5. **Self-care and lifestyle changes**: Exercising regularly, maintaining a balanced diet, getting enough sleep, and practicing stress management techniques can be helpful in improving mood and reducing symptoms of depression. depression.

6.1 EVALUATION AND DIAGNOSIS

Diagnosis and evaluation of depression typically involves a comprehensive process that includes gathering information about the patient's symptoms, medical and psychosocial history, as well as performing specific tests to rule out other medical conditions that may be contributing to the symptoms. . Here are some key aspects of diagnosing and evaluating depression:

Diagnosis:

1. **Clinical history**: The healthcare professional collects detailed information about the patient's symptoms, their duration, severity, and how they affect daily life.

2. **Symptom evaluation**: The emotional, physical and cognitive symptoms associated with depression are evaluated, such as persistent sadness, loss of interest, fatigue, changes in sleep, among others.

3. **Diagnostic criteria**: The criteria established in diagnostic manuals, such as the DSM-5 (Diagnostic and Statistical Manual of Mental Disorders) are used to determine whether the patient meets the criteria for major depressive disorder or other depressive disorders.

4. **Ruling out other medical conditions**: Medical tests may be performed to rule out other medical conditions that may be causing or contributing to depressive symptoms.

Assessment:

1. **Clinical interview**: The mental health professional may conduct a clinical interview to obtain detailed information about the patient's history, symptoms, family history, and triggers.

2. **Self-assessment questionnaires**: Standardized questionnaires, such as the Beck Depression Inventory (BDI) or the Geriatric Depression Scale (GDS), can be used to assess the severity of depressive symptoms.

3. **Behavioral observation**: The professional may observe the patient's behavior during the evaluation to identify signs of depression, such as apathy, frequent crying, or irritability.

4. **Multidisciplinary collaboration**: In some cases, it may be necessary to work collaboratively with other health professionals, such as primary care physicians, psychiatrists or psychologists, to perform a comprehensive evaluation and provide appropriate treatment.

6.2   TREATMENT APPROACHES

The treatment of depression can be approached from different approaches, and often the combination of several methods turns out to be the most effective strategy. Here are some common approaches used in the treatment of depression:

1. **Cognitive behavioral therapy (CBT)**: This approach focuses on identifying and changing negative thought patterns and behaviors that contribute to depression.

2. **Drug Therapy**: The use of antidepressants may be recommended by a mental health professional to help balance chemicals in the brain that are linked to depression.

3. **Interpersonal therapy**: Focuses on improving interpersonal relationships and addressing communication problems that may be contributing to depression.

4. **Supportive Therapy**: Provides a safe space for people to share their feelings and experiences, and receive emotional support from a therapist or support group.

5. **Complementary Therapies**: Some people find benefits in complementary therapies such as meditation, yoga, acupuncture or light therapy.

6. **Physical exercise**: Regular physical activity can help improve mood and reduce symptoms of depression.

7. **Lifestyle care**: Maintaining a healthy lifestyle that includes a balanced diet, sufficient rest and sleep, and avoiding alcohol and drug use can be beneficial in the treatment of depression

Depression is a serious medical condition that usually requires treatment by mental health professionals. While alternative therapies are not a substitute for conventional treatment, some people find certain alternative therapies useful to complement standard treatment. Here are some alternative therapies that some people have found helpful for depression:

1. **Art Therapy**: Art therapy can help express emotions and promote self-expression.

2. **Meditation and mindfulness **: Meditation and mindfulness can help reduce stress and anxiety, which are common in depression.

3. **Acupuncture**: Some people find relief from depressive symptoms through acupuncture, a traditional Chinese medicine approach that involves inserting needles into specific points on the body.

4. **Yoga**: Yoga can be helpful in reducing stress, improving mood, and promoting relaxation.

5. **Herbal Supplements**: Some people find benefit in using herbal supplements such as St. John's Wort to treat depression. However, it is important to speak with a health professional before taking any supplements.

6.3 ALTERNATIVE THERAPY

If you are interested in exploring alternative therapies to treat depression, it is important to remember that these therapies are not a substitute for conventional treatment and that it is essential to consult with a mental health professional before starting any type of therapy. Here are some alternative therapies that some people find helpful:

1. **Cognitive behavioral therapy (CBT)**: Although CBT is a well-established and evidence-supported form of therapy for treating depression, it is considered an alternative therapy for those seeking non-pharmacological approaches. CBT focuses on changing negative thought patterns and unhealthy behaviors.

2. **Light Therapy**: Light therapy, or phototherapy, is often used to treat seasonal affective disorder (SAD), a type of depression related to seasonal changes. Exposure to bright light can help regulate mood and sleep patterns.

3. **Laughter Therapy**: Some people find mood benefits from engaging in laughter therapy, which involves voluntarily laughing to improve emotional and physical health.

4. **Music Therapy**: Music therapy involves the use of music to improve mental and emotional health. Listening to relaxing music or participating in musical activities can help reduce stress and improve mood.

5. **Aromatherapy Therapy**: Some people find mood benefits from using essential oils and engaging in aromatherapy. Some essential oils are believed to have relaxing properties and can help reduce anxiety and stress.

CHAPTER 7

LIVING WITH DEPRESSION

Living with depression can be extremely challenging and affect all aspects of a person's life. Each individual experiences depression uniquely, but in general, people living with depression may experience a combination of the following symptoms:

1. **Feelings of deep and persistent sadness**: An overwhelming feeling of sadness that can persist for weeks, months or even years.

2. **Loss of interest in activities they used to enjoy**: People with depression may lose interest in activities that they previously found pleasurable.

3. **Fatigue and lack of energy**: Depression can cause a constant feeling of fatigue and exhaustion, even after getting enough sleep.

4. **Changes in appetite and weight**: Changes in appetite may arise resulting in significant weight loss or gain.

5. **Sleep problems**: Depression can cause difficulty falling asleep, staying asleep, or waking up early in the morning.

6. **Feelings of worthlessness or guilt**: People with depression may experience feelings of worthlessness, excessive guilt, or self-incrimination.

7. **Difficulties concentrating and making decisions**: Depression can affect the ability to concentrate, remember and make decisions.

8. **Suicidal thoughts**: In severe cases, depression can lead to suicidal thoughts or an increased risk of attempting suicide.

Living with depression can make it difficult to function in daily activities, maintain personal and work relationships, and even care for yourself. It is important to seek professional help if one is experiencing symptoms of depression, as proper treatment can make a big difference in quality of life and mental well-being. Treatment approaches may include psychological therapy, medications, lifestyle changes, and social support.

7.1 SELF-HEALING UDA AND STRATEGI A   COPING

Depression is a serious mental disorder that can profoundly affect a person's life. Below, I will provide you with some coping and self-help strategies that may be helpful in dealing with depression:

1. **Seek professional help**: It is essential to have the support of a mental health professional, such as a psychologist or psychiatrist, to receive an accurate diagnosis and an appropriate treatment plan.

2. **Establish a routine**: Try to maintain a daily routine that includes activities such as getting up early, exercising, eating healthy, and getting enough sleep. A structured routine can help maintain emotional stability.

3. **Practice regular exercise**: Regular physical activity can help improve mood and reduce symptoms of depression. Even a short walk can have positive benefits.

4. **Take care of your diet**: Eating a balanced diet rich in fruits, vegetables, proteins and healthy fats can help maintain physical and mental health.

5. **Maintain social connections**: Although it may be difficult, try to stay in touch with friends and family. Loneliness can make depression worse, so try to maintain meaningful social relationships.

6. **Practice relaxation techniques**: Meditation, deep breathing, yoga or other relaxation techniques can help reduce stress and anxiety.

7. **Set Realistic Goals**: Set achievable goals and break down big tasks into smaller steps. Celebrating achievements, no matter how small, can help boost self-esteem.

8. **Avoid isolation**: If you feel overwhelmed by depression, it is important to seek help and not isolate yourself. Talk to someone you trust or find support groups.

7.2 EMOTIONAL SUPPORT AND SUPPORT NETWORKS

Emotional support and having support networks are essential to facing depression and other emotional challenges. Here are some suggestions on how you can seek out and strengthen your emotional support network:

1. **Family and friends**: Share your feelings with your loved ones. Family and close friends can provide invaluable support and listen to you when you need it.

2. **Support Groups**: Look for local or online support groups where you can share your experiences with people who are going through similar situations. You can find comfort and understanding in these communities.

3. **Health professionals**: Psychologists, psychiatrists, therapists and counselors are trained to provide emotional support and help you manage depression. Don't hesitate to seek professional help if you need it.

4. **Community groups**: Participate in community activities, recreational groups or volunteering. Meeting new people and participating in activities you enjoy can help you build meaningful relationships.

5. **Pets**: The company of a pet can provide comfort and emotional support. Animals can help reduce stress and feelings of loneliness.

6. **Online Resources**: There are online resources, such as support forums, helplines, and mental health apps, that can provide you with emotional support and additional resources.

7. **Self-help and resources**: Read books, articles, and online resources about depression and emotional well-being. You can find useful strategies and tips to help you manage your emotions

7.3   PREVENTION AND RElapses

Preventing depression relapses is crucial to maintaining emotional stability and long-term well-being. Here are some strategies that can help you prevent relapses and better manage depression:

1. **Maintain your treatment**: It is essential to follow the treatment plan recommended by your mental health professional, whether through therapy,   medication or other interventions. Do not stop treatment without consulting your doctor.

2. **Identify your triggers**: Identify the factors that trigger your depressive episodes, such as stress, loneliness, changes in routine, etc. Once identified, look for ways to manage or avoid these triggers.

3. **Practice self-care**: Take time to take care of yourself. This includes maintaining a proper sleep routine, exercising regularly, eating well, practicing relaxation techniques, and activities that you enjoy.

4. **Learn to recognize the warning signs**: Being attentive to the early signs of a relapse can help you intervene in time. If you notice changes in your mood, recurring negative thoughts, or depressive symptoms, seek help immediately.

5. **Establish an action plan**: Together with your mental health professional, create an action plan to deal with a possible relapse. This plan may include specific strategies, such as contacting your therapist, increasing the frequency of sessions, or adjusting medication.

6. **Maintain social connections**: Meaningful social relationships can act as a buffer against depression. Cultivate positive relationships and seek support during difficult times.

7. **Practice resilience**: Learn to manage stress and adapt to life's challenges in a healthy way. Developing coping skills can help you get through difficult situations without falling into depression.

CHAPTER O 8

THE IMPORTANCE   OF SEEKING HELP

Seeking help is essential when facing depression or other mental health issues. Here are some reasons why it is important to seek professional help:

1. **Accurate Diagnosis**: A mental health professional can evaluate your symptoms and provide you with an accurate diagnosis. This is essential to receive appropriate treatment.

2. **Personalized treatment plan**: A professional can develop a personalized treatment plan that fits your specific needs. This may include individual therapy, group therapy, medication, or other interventions.

3. **Emotional support**: Mental health professionals are trained to provide emotional support and help you manage your emotions. They can offer you a safe space to express your feelings and concerns.

4. **Learning coping strategies**: A therapist can teach you coping techniques and strategies to manage depression, reduce stress, and improve your emotional well-being.

5. **Relapse Prevention**: By receiving professional help, you can learn to identify the warning signs of a relapse and develop an action plan to deal with it effectively.

6. **Reducing stigma**: Seeking professional help can help reduce the stigma associated with mental health problems. By talking openly about your difficulties and seeking support, you are helping to   destigmatize   mental health.

7. **Improved quality of life**: By receiving appropriate treatment and support, you can experience a significant improvement in your quality of life. You can learn to manage depression effectively and enjoy a fuller, more satisfying life.

8.1   MENTAL HEALTH PROFESSIONALS

Mental health professionals are experts trained to evaluate, diagnose, and treat a wide range of mental health problems. Here I present some of the most common mental health professionals and their roles:

1. **Psychologist**: A psychologist is a mental health professional who specializes in evaluating and treating emotional and behavioral problems. Psychologists may provide individual therapy, couples therapy, or family therapy to help people manage their emotions and cope with their difficulties.

2. **Psychiatrist**: A psychiatrist is a doctor specialized in the diagnosis, treatment and prevention of mental disorders. Psychiatrists can prescribe psychiatric medications and offer therapy in combination with medication to treat mental health problems.

3. **Clinical Social Worker**: A clinical social worker is a professional who provides emotional support, counseling and resources to individuals, families and groups facing

emotional or social challenges. Clinical social workers can help people access community services and resources.

4. **Counselor or therapist**: Counselors and therapists are professionals trained to provide individual therapy, group therapy, couples therapy, or family therapy. They help people explore their thoughts and emotions, develop coping skills and improve their emotional well-being.

5. **Psychotherapist**: A psychotherapist is a professional who specializes in the practice of psychotherapy, a treatment that involves conversation and emotional work to address mental health problems. Psychotherapists can have different training, such as clinical psychology, psychiatry, clinical social work, among others.

8.2   RESOURCES AND SUPPORTING ORGANIZATIONS

There are numerous resources and support organizations that offer help to people facing mental health issues, including depression. Here are some support organizations and resources that may be helpful:

1. **National Mental Health Agency (NIMH)**: The NIMH is the primary federal mental health research agency in the United States. Their website offers information on various mental disorders, including depression, as well as free resources and publications.

2. **National Alliance on Mental Illness (NAMI)**: NAMI is a community-based organization that provides support, education and advocacy to people affected by mental illness. They offer education programs, support groups, and online resources.

3. **National Suicide Prevention Lifeline**: This organization offers a 24/7 helpline for people in suicidal crisis and their loved ones. They also provide resources and emotional support in times of crisis.

4. **American Psychological Association (APA)**: The APA offers information about mental health, including articles, resources, and tools for finding a psychologist. It also has information on different therapeutic approaches and tips for emotional well-being.

5. **Crisis Text Line**: It is an emotional support service via text message available 24 hours a day for people in crisis. Simply text "HELLO" to 741741 and you will be connected to a trained counselor.

6. **Online Support Groups**: Platforms like 7 Cups of Tea and SupportGroups.com offer professionally moderated online support groups where you can connect with others facing similar challenges.

7. **Community Mental Health Network**: In many communities, there are community mental health centers that offer therapy services, support groups, education, and other resources for people with mental health problems.

8.3 TESTIMONIALS AND PERSONAL EXPERIENCES

Throughout my life I have lived very personal experiences with family members with symptoms of the disease, as well as friends, and it is a traumatic experience that affects you mentally. Seeking professional help is the best alternative to deal with it.

You have to support the person and their environment a lot depression can be anywhere family   country   or   condition   social

CHAPTER 9

THE CAM INO TOWARDS RECOVERY

Recovery from depression is a process that can be unique for each person, as it depends on various factors such as the severity of the depression, the underlying causes, social support, the individual's willingness to seek help and follow a treatment plan. , among others. Here are some general steps that can help on the road to recovery from depression:

1. Recognize depression: The first step is to recognize that you are experiencing depression and accept that you need help to overcome it.

2. Seek professional help: Consult a mental health professional, such as a psychologist, psychiatrist, or counselor, for an accurate diagnosis and appropriate treatment plan.

3. Follow recommended treatment: Follow your mental health professional's recommendations for therapy, medication (if necessary), and other treatments that may be beneficial to you.

4. Adopt a healthy lifestyle: A balanced diet, regular exercise, adequate sleep and stress reduction can help improve your mood and overall well-being.

5. Establish routines: Establishing daily routines can help you maintain structure and emotional stability, which can be especially beneficial during difficult times.

6. Set realistic goals: Set achievable and realistic goals for yourself, both short and long term, and celebrate your achievements, no matter how small.

7. Practice stress management techniques: Learn relaxation techniques, meditation, mindfulness   or other stress management strategies that help you face life's challenges more effectively.

8. Maintain a support network: Talk to friends, family or support groups about your feelings and experiences. Having a support network can be essential in the recovery process.

9.1 STEPS FOR RECOVERY

In the process of recovery from depression, it is important to take concrete steps to improve your emotional and mental well-being. Here are some steps you can take on your path to recovery:

1. **Seek professional help**: Consult a mental health professional, such as a psychologist, psychiatrist, or counselor, to obtain a proper diagnosis and receive guidance on the most appropriate treatment for you.

2. **Follow the treatment plan**: It is important to follow your mental health professional's recommendations regarding therapy, medication (if necessary), and other treatments that have been prescribed for you.

3. **Adopt a healthy lifestyle**: Maintain a balanced diet, exercise regularly, make sure you get enough sleep, and look for ways to reduce stress in your life.

4. **Engage in therapy**: Therapy, whether individual, group or family, can be very beneficial in the recovery process. Through therapy you can explore your thoughts, emotions and behavior patterns, and learn strategies to cope with depression.

5. **Practice self-care techniques**: Spend time doing activities that help you relax and take care of yourself. This may include practicing meditation, yoga, deep breathing, therapeutic writing, or any other activity that helps you feel better.

6. **Set goals and celebrate achievements**: Set realistic goals for yourself and celebrate your achievements, no matter how small. This will help you stay motivated and maintain a positive attitude.

7. **Maintain a support network**: Talk to friends, family, or members of a support group about your feelings and experiences. Having a support network can be essential in the recovery process.

8. **Be patient and compassionate with yourself**: Recovery from depression can take time and effort. Remember to be patient with yourself and treat yourself with kindness and compassion every step of the way.

9.2   MENTAL HEALTH MAINTENANCE

Maintaining mental health is essential for long-term emotional and psychological well-being. Here I present some practices and habits that can help you take care of your mental health:

1. **Regular exercise**: Regular physical exercise not only benefits your physical health, it can also improve your mood, reduce stress and anxiety, and increase self-esteem.

2. **Healthy eating**: A balanced and nutritious diet can have a positive impact on your mental health. Eating nutrient-dense foods like fruits, vegetables, whole grains, lean proteins, and healthy fats can help you feel better both physically and emotionally.

3. **Adequate sleep**: Getting enough sleep and getting a good rest is crucial to maintaining mental health. Try to establish a regular sleep routine and make sure you get the rest you need each night.

4. **Relaxation practices**: Incorporating relaxation techniques such as meditation, deep breathing, yoga or visualization can help you reduce stress, anxiety and improve your emotional well-being.

5. **Set limits**: Learn how to set healthy boundaries in your personal and professional relationships to avoid emotional exhaustion and protect your mental health.

6. **Seek social support**: Maintaining healthy and meaningful social connections is important for mental health. Talking to friends, family, or a therapist can provide you with emotional support and a space to share your worries.

7. **Manage stress**: Learn to identify your sources of stress and develop effective strategies to manage it, such as planning, organizing, problem solving, and practicing self-compassion.

8. **Stay mentally active**: Stimulate your mind with activities that challenge you intellectually, such as reading, learning something new, solving riddles or   puzzles , or participating in creative activities.

9. **Seek professional help if necessary**: If you feel that your mental health is being affected, do not hesitate to seek help from a mental health professional, such as a psychologist or psychiatrist, to receive appropriate support and treatment.

Remember that taking care of your mental health is an ongoing process that requires constant attention and effort. Incorporating these healthy habits into your daily life can help you maintain a healthy and balanced mind.

9.3   THE ROLE OF FAMILY AND FRIENDS

Family and friends play a vital role in a person's emotional well-being and mental health. Your support, understanding and presence can be key in times of difficulty. Here I present some important aspects about the role of family and friends in mental health:

1. **Emotional Support**: Family and friends can provide significant emotional support to a person who is going through difficult times, such as a mental disorder. Listening, showing empathy and being present are important ways to support someone who is struggling with their mental health.

2. **Support network**: Having a strong support network can help reduce social isolation and feelings of loneliness, factors that can worsen mental health problems. Family and friends can be part of this support network, offering company, affection and understanding.

3. **Open Communication**: Open and honest communication with family and friends can facilitate the expression of feelings, thoughts and concerns related to mental health. Feeling heard and understood can be very comforting for someone who is going through a difficult time.

4. **Foster a supportive environment**: It is important that family and friends foster an environment of support and understanding, free of stigma and judgment, where the person feels safe to talk about their mental health problems without fear to be judged.

5. **Participating in recovery**: Family and friends can play an active role in the recovery of a loved one who is struggling with mental health issues. They can provide practical help, accompaniment to medical appointments, remembering to take medications, among other forms of support.

6. **Education and awareness**: It is important for family and friends to become informed and educated about mental disorders to better understand the needs and challenges of their loved one. Raising mental health awareness can help reduce stigma and improve support.

CHAPTER 10

FINAL THOUGHTS

Depression is a serious mental disorder that can profoundly affect a person's life, as well as their loved ones. Here are some final thoughts on depression:

1. **Depression does not define a person**: It is important to remember that depression is a medical condition, not a character trait. A person who struggles with depression is not weak or less valuable than others. It is crucial to separate the illness from the identity of the person experiencing it.

2. **The importance of seeking help**: Depression is treatable, and seeking professional help is essential for recovery. There is no need to be afraid or ashamed to ask for help. Talking to a mental health professional can make a difference in the recovery process.

3. **Community support is essential**: Depression can be a heavy burden to carry, but it should not be faced alone. Support from family, friends, mental health professionals, and the broader community can be instrumental on the road to recovery.

4. **Self-care is essential**: Taking care of yourself is essential for mental health. Incorporating healthy habits into your daily routine, finding activities that bring joy and well-being, and setting healthy boundaries are important aspects of self-care.

5. **Hope and perseverance are key**: Although depression can seem overwhelming at times, it is important to remember that recovery is possible. Maintaining hope, being patient with yourself, and persevering in the treatment process are key aspects of overcoming depression.

6. **Awareness and education are key**: Education about depression and other mental disorders can help reduce stigma and foster understanding and support for those struggling with these issues. Raising awareness is the first step towards creating a more compassionate and empathetic society.

10.1 MESSAGE AND HOPE

Dear friend,

In the dark moments of life, when depression clouds your mind and your heart feels overwhelmed, I want to remind you that hope always shines somewhere inside you, even when you can't see it clearly right now.

Depression can seem like a lonely and exhausting journey, but you are not alone in this battle. There are people who love you, who care about you, and who want to see you overcome this challenge. Don't be afraid to ask for help, share your thoughts and feelings, and seek the support you need.

Remember that depression does not define who you are. You are valuable, worthy of love and deserving of a full and happy life. Recovery is possible, and every small step you take forward brings you a little closer to the light at the end of the tunnel.

Keep hope in your heart, cultivate patience with yourself and trust that with time, treatment and effort, you will be able to overcome this storm and find the calm and peace you long for.

Don't hesitate to seek help, take care of yourself, and remember that you deserve to feel good about yourself. Life has a lot to offer you, and I am confident that you can overcome this challenge and find the happiness you deserve.

With love and hope,

Franky Arango

10.2 CLOSING AND CONCLUSIONS

Over the course of our conversation about depression, we have explored various aspects related to this mental condition, including the recognition of depression, steps towards recovery, the role of family and friends, as well as final thoughts and a message of hope.

Depression is a common mental illness that can affect people of all ages, genders, and backgrounds. It is important to recognize the symptoms of depression and seek professional help when necessary. Recovery from depression can be a challenging process, but it is possible with the right treatment, support from loved ones, and a comprehensive approach to mental health care.

Support from family and friends plays a crucial role in the emotional well-being of a person struggling with depression. Open communication, emotional support, and understanding are critical to helping someone overcome the challenges of depression.

It is important to remember that depression does not define a person and that hope is always present, even in the darkest moments. Education, awareness, and actively seeking help are important steps on the road to recovery.

Ultimately, mental health is a fundamental aspect of our overall well-being, and taking care of our mental health is just as important as taking care of our physical health. Let us remember that we are not alone in our fight against depression and that there is always help and hope available for those who seek it.

If you are struggling with depression or know someone who is, don't hesitate to reach out for help and support. With patience, treatment and the right support, it is possible to overcome depression and move forward towards a full and   long life.

THANKS

In the journey of life, we encounter challenges that test us, push us to the limits of our strength, and plunge us into an abyss of darkness and desolation. In those moments of hopelessness and pain, is when we discover the true strength of our spirit and the light that shines in the depths of our soul. It is in those moments of crisis and confusion where faith becomes our refuge, hope our driving force and love our salvation.

"A Monster Called Depression" is much more than a book; It is the testimony of an internal battle, the chronicle of a fight against the shadows of the soul and the narrative of a victory over adversity. In each page of this work, pain and anguish are reflected, but also courage, perseverance and the light that emerges from the darkness.

On this journey of self-discovery and healing, I have been blessed with the unwavering support of my children, Juan Javier and Angélica Liliana. Your unconditional love, your deep understanding and your constant presence have been the pillar on which I have built my strength, the foundation from which I have raised my voice and the inspiration that has guided my pen.

To God, source of all life and love, I raise my deepest gratitude for illuminating my path, for supporting me in moments of weakness and for allowing me to be an instrument of hope and healing for those who fight against the monster of depression. In His infinite mercy and love, I have found comfort, strength, and renewal.

To my children, Angélica Liliana and Juan Javier earthly angels who have been my light in the darkness, I owe them my eternal gratitude. Your loving presence, your tireless wisdom, and your unwavering support have been my rock in the midst of the storm, my lighthouse in the storm, and my reason to move forward.

On this journey of self-discovery and healing, I have learned that love is the antidote to pain, faith is the shelter in the storm, and hope is the light that guides our path. In every word of this book, in every page written with tears and smiles, in every verse impregnated with truth and passion, the echo of my gratitude, my love and my commitment to be light in the darkness, hope in despair and love resonate. in the loneliness.

"A Monster Called Depression" is the testimony of a struggle, but also of a victory; It is the narrative of pain, but also of a contribution to society